LOST AND FOUND

Selected Poems and Translations of

DAVID MARCUS

LOST AND FOUND
First published 2007
by New Island
2 Brookside
Dundrum Road
Dublin 14
www.newisland.ie

ISBN 978-1-905494-72-9

Book design by Inka Hagen
Printed in the UK by Athenaeum Press Ltd., Gateshead, Tyne & Wear

New Island received financial assistance from
The Arts Council (An Chomhairle Ealaíon), Dublin, Ireland.

10 9 8 7 6 5 4 3 2 1

Contents

Translations

Introduction

Novelist, autobiographer, anthologist, short-story writer, and of course editor *extraordinaire* – what a life of words David Marcus has made! It's hard to think of another figure in twentieth-century Irish literary life to whom the designation 'man of letters' is better suited. In ways that have been as unselfish as they have been influential, David has truly been a person of the book.

His influence is part of the history of the growth and development of Irish writing over the past forty years or so. Very few Irish writers in that period have not been indebted to David for not only their first appearance in print – an invaluable boost to confidence in itself – but for continued support, interest, goodwill and practical suggestions. Typically, David would not think of himself as an influential figure. And his unselfishness has ensured that there's no school of Marcus – in fact, that would be the very last thing he would wish for. Look at his work as a short-story anthologist, though, and see how consistently the standards of open-mindedness and variety are maintained, standards which are not only well worth keeping up as a general principle but which have been active and attractive features of the fiction that has come to the fore beginning in the 1970s. Or, to take another tack, consider the way a Marcus anthology is put together; the subtle sequencing, the interplay of light and dark thematic matters, the rhythm of the whole. There's a touch of the poet in that tact, that sense of timing.

And now we can see that touch in its proper medium.

That's right. In addition to his many other literary accomplishments, David Marcus is also a poet, and indeed as a young man devoted a good deal of his literary energies to verse – was at the time 'convinced,' as he ruefully records in *Oughtobiography*, 'I was the best unpublished poet in Ireland under twenty-one'. Reading that, it's difficult not to be reminded of Jacob Cohen, the young medical student who frets to plight his troth in rhyme to Deirdre Buckley in David's 1986 novel *A Land in Flames*. A portrait of the novelist as a young man? The dates don't fit. But the essentials do: the lure of beauty, and the passion and hunger for attachment. Unpublished he may have been, but not for long; a number of the poems included in the present selection appeared in periodicals of national and international repute – *Envoy, Rann, Georgia Review*, the *Adelphi*; not to mention *Six Poems* published by the Dolmen Press in 1952.

Making this publishing occasion more piquant is the fact that renewed acquaintance with David Marcus's poetry is due, in the first place, to an accident. Or rather, to two. The first was safely tidying the poems away in an attaché case, so they wouldn't be lost, only for them to be left where they lay for years, forgotten. Then, some eighteen months or so ago, in the chance rediscovery of their resting place, they came to light again. If, as Wordsworth has it, the child is father to the man, we can only imagine what a complicated recognition scene it was when the man in his eighties heard the youth of sixty years ago speak his heart again. Especially when we remember that that youth's preoccupation with belonging, acceptance and equal footing, for all their romantic colouration, contain an additional, perhaps now more audible resonance of the strange wartime conditions in which they first were written.

The story of poetry and David Marcus is not confined to his writing it, of course. As founder and editor (with Terence Smith) of *Irish Writing* he provided space for what at this remove is pretty much a who's who of Irish poets at mid-century. To mention merely the most illustrious, Louis MacNeice, John Hewitt, Patrick Kavanagh, Anthony Cronin, Thomas Kinsella, John Montague were all contributors. This was at a time when poetry definitely needed a hand – *Irish Writing* first appeared in 1946. And that the hand was extended from Cork is another not insignificant piece of evidence that Irish post-war culture was not quite as down and out as has often been alleged. Not only that, but in 1948 David founded *Poetry Ireland*, which went on to enjoy a second life as a regular supplement in *Irish Writing*. His continuing editorial generosity to his own generation has its most obvious embodiment in the anthology *Irish Poets 1924–1974*, in the introduction to which an 'to order their own affairs ... free of the original sin of subjugation' is credited with the inauguration of a distinctive, post-Yeatsian, 'era of modern Irish poetry (Mark II).' These words of tribute, and the value they place on independence of mind and action, expressed though they are in a seemingly glancing manner, touch on matters fundamental not only to the development of a literature but to an appreciation of qualities within David's own Jewish heritage.

Another signal service to poetry which David carried out was the inclusion of poems on his celebrated 'New Irish Writing' page in *The Irish Press*. It was exciting enough when David accepted a story of mine. But its appearance cheek-by-jowl with a Derek Mahon poem had me completely over the moon. Yet, for all his various attentions to the muse, it is as a translator of poetry that David Marcus made his most visible mark. Of Irish poetry, that is; and of *The Midnight Court* in particular. And indeed from *Oughtobiography* we learn that there seems to have been a link between his being drawn to Brian Merriman's poem and the release of his own poetic flow. His immersion in the task of translating from the Irish in general was a source of considerable stimulus, pleasure and intellectual challenge for the young poet. To cite *Oughtobiography* again:

> ... not being a native speaker or a Gaelic scholar, my enjoyment of translating Irish poetry was to a great extent para-physical. It always gave me a sense of elation that was more than just spiritual. The sheer hard work, the trial and error of seeking to reproduce as faithfully as possible the vital statistics of a poem was a thoroughly exhausting struggle.

Good training. The structures, metrics and rhythms of traditional Irish verse are certainly audible in the poems that follow.

But *The Midnight Court* ... a risky undertaking to publish it in translation. Frank O'Connor's 1945 version had been banned. It was precisely for that reason that David decided to go ahead with his own version, and with the encouragement of Liam Miller it was published in 1953. Lo and behold, this event was not the end of civilisation as certain local worthies knew it – or, rather, as they wanted it to be known. It might even be said to have acted as a little breakthrough, although that was not confirmed for sure until a stage version, written by David and Sean

McCann, was put on at the Gate in 1968 to packed houses. I didn't mention that David is a playwright too ...

The poems from the Irish included in *Lost and Found* have a certain amount in common with David's original poems, not only technically, as mentioned above, but thematically. One obvious case in point is the interest in passion shared by poems across the board, an interest which gains additional piquancy from being located in such arguably unexpected places as the verse of Geoffrey Keating and Patrick Pearse. Not that the interest is indulged for its own sake, or merely out of prurience. On the contrary, it opens into broad perspectives on such concerns as the trials of love, the fate of the body, the impact of loss, the exhilaration and precariousness of being carried away and the sobriety and inevitability of coming back down to earth. And such concerns are the property of all poetry, old and new, regardless of tradition or tongue. Desire and its turbulence exert their irresistible allure. But aftermath and isolation very often have the last word. This word – signature of a lost world – is all the more resonant when it sounds in poems such as 'Fratricide' and 'Exiled' in which private experience yields, without surrendering, to the wartime context in which the poems were written.

There is a sense in which the poet seems to be very much alive to Wordsworth's dictum that poems are 'emotions recollected in tranquillity', while at the same time being equally sensitive to the knowledge that tranquillity is pretty hard to come by. Even so, if these poems frequently feature heavy weather, emotional and otherwise, they seldom make heavy weather of it. Their tone, often confessional, is almost always civil; their disposition invariably inclines towards tolerance. And, as their sound stanzaic structures and fitting rhymes remind us, there is an interest in balance here, in attempts at reconciliation, and there's an intuitive sympathy for the other side of the story. Readers will hardly be surprised to learn that David is a skilled pianist, seeing here how well white notes speak to black and with how light a touch the overall sense is conveyed. The touch of the poet.

Lightness is not necessarily synonymous with 'light verse', though; as W.H. Auden pointed out, 'light verse can be serious'. His point derives from the second of the three criteria for inclusion in the *Oxford Book of Light Verse*: 'Poetry intended to be read, but having for its subjectmatter the everyday social life of its period or the experiences of the poet as an ordinary human being.' That last clause is the one worth dwelling on here. The common lot, the broad view, our fragile destinies make up David Marcus's poetic realm; uplift and downfall, intensity and emptiness, fervour and stoicism. The palette with which this realm is painted consists of the basic colours of night and day, and the poems resemble sketches in charcoal, outlines fraught with implication.

It has been a wonderful surprise to find that these poems have made it through the years. But it has been no surprise at all to discover their contents. All who have had the good fortune of knowing David Marcus will recognise at once his human, and humane, spirit here. Those who may not know him, soon will, and will be glad.

George O'Brien

Seduction

Bring me tonight a lover clean
A lover pure, without a stain
Whose soul is guiltless of all sin
Whose skin is white, pure white whose skin.

Lay him beside me in my bed
Beside me lay his smiling head
And close his eyes when he is laid
And he is laid when he is dead.

And I will procure a resurrection
Breathing his life, his living breath
And breathing to him that breath is Death
And Death a beautiful creation.

Breasts, rise ye up, rise up ye breasts
Swollen to nipple-point your purpose
Shall he explore between my breasts?
Shall he disturb his virgin poise?

His hand shall find my naked parts
His hand shall find me naked, parts
Of me beneath his hands shall find
The truth, the truth his hands shall find.

And none but he shall know I prayed
To have a lover without sin
Shall know 'twas him my love betrayed
Whose skin was white, white was whose skin.

I will have done with him by dawn
My maids will come to turn him out
And I will turn and turn about
And muse until the sun is warm.

Enter a Spirit

Come through the wall
Be shrouded in secrecy
I will come that way too in time to come.
Break through my will
Spilling the ancient heresy
Of thought, the traitor to the rule of thumb.

Come as you please,
Time is no part of life;
Thought and time and the mind are traitors three.
Look. I say look;
Sound well that silver laugh,
Laughter or words will do now equally.

Words? I could talk
Now at the end of all;
Words, always words; action was needed most.
So I should take
In my hands your face so pale.
I would; but how can someone love a ghost?

Poem

Love cannot hold me out much more of hope
whose part is read before the play is done.
Like pebbles perched upon a windy slope
they cannot alter course once they've begun
although the hill may end in ditch or wall.

Hands eyes and heart may fasten on your face
and hips do well to hold your lips in thrall
            – but all they can accomplish is a kiss.

Our minds can act their part upon the stage,
our bodies' joy can give to love its day,
but these performances will not assuage
the troubled wound that bleeds throughout the play.

Loving our best there still will always be
the soul's continuing virginity.

Sonnet

For thee, my love, a lifelong lease on Time,
Safe passage through the crumbling Halls of Life,
Eternal stay in the most temperate clime,
And clear exemption from dark Age's knife.
If I could garner knowledge from the air
Or by some strange or subtle alchemy
Compound a wine that has of each a share,
If needs, I'd bring it in my hands to thee.
The sweetest verse should every day be spoken.
Your face by every person should be seen.
Your form for other beauty might have been.
It's easy known my love could not be such,
Even so, yet still I love you much too much.

The Animal

O animal that was my past,
my present, and my days to come,
over the far horizon fast
you vanished from my eager gun.

O animal that I did stalk,
that took me from the grip of night,
drilling me to the hunter's walk,
paring my vision to his sight.

You brought me on your unknown road
and made me track you to your lair,
made for the kill, as though there flowed
some doom between us through the air.

And then you stopped and turned your eyes,
I felt me naked while you stared;
why was your beauty a surprise?
what was the power I had dared?

You fired the shot. Yours was the brain
that willed the finish from the start.
How could mine own two hands have slain
the animal within my heart?

Punchinello

I swore I had the perfect one,
       The very one, the only one,
The one to love and love me true
       For all my lifelong days.

But I was wrong and I was left –
       Forlorn, dejected, and bereft –
With empty thoughts and heart half-cleft
       And wildness in my gaze.

The size of her, the eyes of her,
       But oh the guile and lies of her,
I thought I'd made a prize of her,
       I thought I was a king.

But crown was lost, and throne was lost,
       And sceptre, sway, and court were lost
And queen was lost – and there I was,
       An ordinary thing.

True, that's all past, it's history;
       I've no one now to worry me.
To see me talk and acting free
       You'd think I couldn't care.

But sometimes when the night is cold
       And half the moon is pale and old,
I build myself a fire of gold,
       And sit like this and stare.

The Ten Roads to My Love

The ten roads to my love
Were hung with coloured lanterns,
And people went out dancing
On the ten roads to my love.

They drove the hills before them
And tore aside the bushes,
They made the roads a carpet
And granted all my wishes.

At every corner-crossing
They had a guide await me,
And when I reached the castle
They sent my love to greet me.

And the ten roads to my love
They silenced for our loving,
And lingered at the entrance
To cheer me on my leaving.

How happy was their laughter,
How simple-souled their joy;
They thanked me and they blessed me,
And what could I reply?

How could I know their praises
Were mockery and tricks
To drive me from their city
And never have me back?

And that on my returning
They'd block my every move?
That guards and barricades would fill
The ten roads to my love?

Barriers

Had we the least of nights to make amends
For all the different ways we have to go,
How quick we'd be to do as much, and so
That least of nights we would be more than friends.

But now between us is uncoiled a strand
That either time or space can break asunder,
And when a thought of you is all my wonder
I know not where along it is your hand.

This talk is lover's talk – but it uncovers
Storm-clouds of truth that harry us like rain;
We might as well be vagabonds in Spain
As be the way we are – the ghosts of lovers.

Mind and Matter

My darling, as down we lie
our bodies grappled each to each
we cannot take love leisurely
for we have heard the body's speech,
but answering its urgent call
is not so easy nor so clear
when minds must think away the wall
'twixt what we may and may not dare;
so when we hope our passion's tamed
by mind's dispassionate restriction,
secretly it has become inflamed,
bruised by the flesh's contradiction;
love is like having love on loan
when body cannot body own.

Love's House

If, sometimes, argument
Should eat into our love,
Remember love is lent
To us, and we must prove
Not only that we're worth
The haven of its home
But that we can unearth
The subtle, silent worm
Which breeds about its base
A hateful, piercing wit
That undermines love's house
If we abandon it.
Accordingly, if words
Escape from us in rage
Like wild, unsightly birds
That have escaped their cage,
And lure us from love's house
In scurrying pursuit,
Let's ask this question: is
Love's charity and truth
Something that we can leave
When we grow mad or bored
And then reclaim when we've
Grown bored with being bored?
No – for within love's house
It lives, and cannot quit,
And it will stay with us
If we will stay with it.

Therefore let us retrace
Our steps along the way –
For in the worthless chase
We are the real prey –
And let us find once more
That sanctified abode
Or ever-open door,
The real house of God,
Love's house, a house of peace,
Which we may have and keep,
Where gaiety's increase
We may for ever reap;
Within that house alone,
Secure from argument,
We can begin to own
The love that we are lent,
And each day set apart
Our special, daily goal:
A holiday in the heart,
And a sabbath in the soul.

Day and Night

Why has the day no spirit
But an angry useless mood?
It has not a heart to inspire it;
Its poems and lovers are crude.

But take Night: there's a woman of beauty,
A colour of mystical hue
Whose darkness makes light of its bounty,
Yet remaining perpetually new.

And why wonder? Why think it a puzzle,
Or presume to consider it odd?
For Day's but the Mind of the Mighty,
While Night is the Heart of God.

Conscripts

This is the kind of night
when trees are the people I hate
who run their hands through my hair

when footsteps just melt at my touch
of girls who are everywhere
and walk through a door to the moon

when shadows have less of care
than cats on a skull-top roof
that peel the skin from my fear

and frog-march my thoughts to fight
for a prize that my heart cannot share;
this is that kind of a night.

There and Back

We leant upon the quay-wall,
The sea-wall, falling
Down to the waves where the moon lay soaked.
And the brave, bright light
Of the fair was calling,
But we leant upon the wall and we talked and smoked.

The sun that shone
Was gone from Currabinny
And the night had come like the echo of a sound;
But her one shrill thrill
Wasn't worth my lonely money,
Be it tuppence or a tanner or a penny or a pound.

So we turned like cowards
Towards the hidden village;
Was it shame that slowed our paces or the darkness of the track?
Like a vile thought caught
Till it snapped the muscles' message –
For a moment we could neither carry onward nor go back.

For a moment – then,
Again our faces turning,
We ran towards the quayside thinking only of the fair;
But the brave, bright light
No longer now was burning,
The gates were shut and bolted; nobody was there.

Night in a Neutral Country

Night falls at last
In stuttered silences,
Shadows are folded upon sleeping grass;
I peer
To catch this solemn, tender Is,
And pin it to the memory that was.

Sounds from the sky
I hear;
But not of 'planes.
Clouds roll, but not by wingèd monsters tossed.
Midnight in veils upon the city rains,
And street-lamps shine
Unbridled through the frost.

Shall I believe there is a ranker clime
Where darkness hides the palsied bones of youth;
And tender Night
Sends Death to squash their prime?
I must believe it; or I gainsay truth.

Exiled

Memory walks a lonely road,
Reaches a village in the mind
Where doors are shut, and flags are still,
And children sullen and unkind.

This is the place where once we came
And found a people who would aid
Our youthful love, and prize our joy;
This is the place where once we stayed.

And when we left they said, 'Return,
Return again to greet your own.'
But now they recognise me not,
Because I have returned alone.

Fratricide

My people come from a far-off land
And bear the mark of the burning-brand.

But words are useless. They do not speak.
My people turned the other cheek.

Who are my people? I search my mind
And remember Donne who was all mankind.

And the frontiers are crossed so I may as well face it –
The world is my lover. I rush to embrace it.

But the world is no woman and less of a man,
And my people are worse now than when they began.

Worse indeed. It is clear there is nothing to save
For I see that my people are digging my grave.

Two Birds

The day hadn't quite known what to do
Till just about twilight, and the two
Old birds that lived in the tree so long
Jerked up their heads and stopped their song,
And flew away.
      As quick as that.
I had no chance to notice what
Had scared them, or if anything had,
Though I was quite a knowing lad
Where birds were concerned; I had watched them nights
And learned the reason for all their flights.
But this one stumped me – at least until
The sun had gone and a sudden chill
Crept up the lanes and climbed the wall
And covered the barn and the house and all –

Until a noise like the roll of a drum
Came up from the fields. It seemed to have come
From the fields although it was thunder of course,
And the rain – I had never seen rain with such force!
I stood watching it pour; I'd forgotten the tree
And the birds that had gone and where they might be,
And just then, as I gazed, there was one mighty crash
And the farm was ablaze with a wonderful flash.
I'd have thought 'twas enough to burn everything down
The crops and the farmhouse and even the town –

But instead I could swear it took aim at the tree
It aimed and it cut it as clean as could be,
And then it blew up. The tree seemed to fall
Rather slowly as if it might not after all,
But it did.
      When the sound of its fall died away
The silence was heavy and hard, and the grey
Of the sky was quite bare. And again, just like that,
I heard sounds and I looked, and just about at
The tree-stump where the cinders were hissing and steaming
The birds had returned, very angry and screaming.

Night, the Toper

By now the sun had run away, and half a day and half
    a day
Had grumbled and refused to stay, and fields were left
    to dream.
And bowls of light the night had drained, and none
    complained and none complained
When such a sot bent down and stained the skyline's
    silver seam.
But there he was, and as I swear, he wandered here and
    wandered there
And fixed us all with ghoulish stare and croaked a
    mournful tune;
And just to see what he could do, (since stars were one
    or two or few),
He puffed and blowed until he blew a bleary-looking
    moon.
He danced and played and made the night a night-long
    skite without respite
Until the very clouds were tight and soon began to
    yawn;
And then – the knave – he gave a 'lep' and put a step
    beyond a step
And walked away and left a most disreputable dawn!

Trees in a Storm

The comings and goings of the wounded wind
Disturb the trees that sentinel the lawn
Making them wander nervously about
Anxious to hear the bugle of the dawn;

And then a sudden gust whips them around
Like rifles cocked their branches come unfurled,
Crowding together, terror at their roots,
They shout 'Who goes there?' to an empty world.

Death of a Sailor

The long man from the sea
Fell up the golden shore
Cried his eyes on the sands
Singing 'I'll sail no more.'

'I'll sail no more the waves;
And what will happen me?
I'll die on land.' So said
The song man from the sea.

He took off his cap of braid
And took off his silken shirt
He took out his singing knife
And dug a grave for his mirth.

He stretched himself there and then
And went through a form of grace
A wave broke over his heart
And a wave broke over his face.

Slowly the place was filled
With waves from far and wide
But he lay on his back for a song
Blowing bubbles till he died.

The Lighthouse

Returning, late at night, the cliff was lit
By sudden rays a reeling lighthouse threw;
They pressed against the flowers as if they knew
Some mischief had been done, and knew that it
Was hidden there and trembling in its core.

I walked with quickened step and turned my eyes
Away from them, or tried to wear the mask
Of innocence in case they'd think to ask
Where I had been, and all my hobbled lies
Would only serve to make them question more.

But they had burnt their way into my mind
And touched off little horrors at my feet
And made me run in panic through the street
Like some poor hunted convict who must find
Without delay an unwatched, open door.

Modern Times

The day is a vast machine
Pressing out slabs of time.
Parcelled in shiny paper
Ready for Man sublime;
Opened in fevered haste
Wasted in slothful prime;
The day is a vast machine
Pressing out slabs of time.

The night is a dull incision
And useless for the wise.
The virgin's fearful prison
The prostitute's assize;
The lovers' mad collision
The millionaire's demise;
The night is a dull incision
But useless for the wise.

Oh, war's a passing fancy
And sex a foolish fad.
And living is a riddle
That drives the artist mad.
And birth is rather silly
But death is rather sad.
And all that's not is sainted
And all that is is bad.

Return of an Army

Trample of soldier;
Rumble of gun;
Bunting and banterole
Obliterate sun.

Who's for the Desk, boys?
Who will be Chief?
Who's for the roadside,
And who for relief?

In ghostlier regions
Far from our aid,
Those who escaped all this
Hold their parade.

Their consummation
Is our confusion,
While our's – our's is
Their disillusion.

A soldier approached me
And asked for a job.
How could I tell him
I hadn't a bob?

So, mangle the Desks, boys,
And strangle the Chief.
We'll sit on the roadside
And wait for relief.

The Shell

A shell can carry all I know
Of sand and sea and sky;
Can set them upon mountain-snow
And leave the mountain dry;
Can bathe a night of emptiness
In pools of silver light
As once it bathed the silver pools
With seven kinds of night.

With all I know of sand and sky
And all I know of sea,
The champion of hurricanes
Can't match my history;
Can't raise a breeze within the shell
I place upon my palm,
Though all his wintry worlds combine
My world is firm and calm.

This is the simple miracle
Of sky and sea and sand
I listen to from day to day
To try to understand
The true perspective of all things,
The rich and artless spell
That binds the world outside unto
The world within the shell.

Jumbo

What pity is in your eyes?
Pity for you or us?
That we are not your size
Or that you are so tremendous?

And when you lift your trunk
And trumpet through the air,
Do you mean it as a song
Of triumph or despair?

We cannot tell the thoughts
That hide out in your brain,
Or whether you have forgotten
Jungles African and Indian.

Like you, we are bewildered,
And wander off the tracks;
Like you we lumber,
Children perched upon our backs.

A Great Man's Famous Ways

A great man's famous ways
Have made me less a man
Than the most aimless days
We've had since you began
To reconstruct my heart
Out of some words and looks
That never were a part
Of a great man's famous books.

He wrote about his youth
Modelled by distant suns,
And how he quarried truth
Beneath the legs of guns,
Till he had measured fame
To fit him like a glove
And children spoke his name;
He never wrote of love.

How would he grow so wise
With no one in his life
To put against the lies
Of medals, talk, and strife?
And what's his mighty age
If he cannot retrace
A time when in his rage
He babbled for a face?

What is it then I gain
By making you a rhyme
If it should not remain
When we have quitted Time?
I gain all that is best
Of our own lives and love;
The praises of the rest
Are over and above.

Words

Why should I put in words
What I shall have to forget,
If not that my thoughts are snared
Already in your net?

Why should I strive to tell
My soul's most secret part,
If not that you have built
Its mysterious heart?

What can I make you know
Because two words may rhyme?
A poet cannot prove
With rhyming words his love.

Portrait

Hitting the bottle every other night,
Having it easy with women, betting on the nod,
He rode his youth to death against the years
Till one day he got thinking about God.

Then not so much the Deity as his own soul –
Something his fuddled brain could bring to court –
But hadn't he been a ticket ? was his thought
As Conscience gabbled out the long report.

The point was when, not how, to change the act;
(How to be good everybody knew);
Could he be really that hard-pressed for time?
Like toy balloons the fears within him grew.

And like balloons they burst upon his will
Making him long for drink or long for bed;
He wanted neither and he wanted both,
He tried to rub the pain out of his head.

Eventually he slept, his last thought being
One of relief to leave it all behind.
But in his sleep devilish dreams continued
Blowing the same balloons up in his mind.

The Winter of Love

Clouds came down from the clouds to walk the pavements,
And I called after them, my hardy friends,
Who took my love away in a closed pavilion
And set her counting the hours till daylight ends.

She picked up the yellow folds of her dress of goldness
And marshalled the bluebells out of the growing corn;
Oh bright in the dark was the hue of that distant gladness
As red as the blood that clamours to kiss the thorn.

In the night we had found how the branches of love are laden
With fruit that is ripe for the thief or the wolf to destroy,
And her body was blessed like an orchard that reaches its season
And leans to the fingers that gather the weight of its joy.

The day I awoke to the lure of that miracle harvest
I planted an acre with seeds of perennial flame,
And the sun brought them splendidly forth like a chorus of dance
That spattered the landscape with colours her magic would name.

I walked to the headland and lay with my back to the labour
And measured the weather that argued to climb my arms,
And a blade of its grass could have opened a road to my centre
That hungered to empty its hiveful of love in swarms.

But swiftly the blight had descended to wander my Eden,
And tattered the garments that covered my angel's breast;
The touch of her skin was a serpent encircling my body,
The fork of her kisses had branded my lips with their crest.

O now I may wander the fields of a savage location
And curse at the scarecrows that cherish these ugly lands,
But all I can reap is the poisonous hail of the morning
That murdered my loved one and rotted the soil in my hands.

Under the Heaven's Summer Roof

Under the heaven's summer roof
the massive double-visioned moon
falls like a hand, the hand of one
whose power was never overthrown.

The trees, with lifeless leaves, enjoy
the heavier arms of summer's night,
forgetting winter's going-forth
and snow that held their roots and earth.

It all is part and parcel of
places that never seem to change;
last year and next are similar
and seasonable photographs.

And every echo of the past –
the half-built wall, the broken shed,
the laneway growing dark with dread,
were life-long tenants from the start.

Except where, ghost-like and afraid,
a presence waits for each return,
the end of every circle made,
the centre of our cause to mourn.

Words to that Effect

A poet writes a love-song –
Or words to that effect –
And love-song follows love-song
Attempting to dissect
With surgical precision
And comprehensive view
The poem from the passion,
The tender from the true.

Every exploration
Probes the mystery
Of love's exact relation
To life's reality;
The poet's skill, however,
Provides no certain cure
For the recurrent fever
His own love must endure.

As physic for the terror
Of knowing love can die
A poem is an error
At best, at worst a lie;
Its pallid, adjectival
Drip may gain small time,
But love has no survival
In an ambulance of rhyme.

A Tributary Sonnet

I waked upon the land and ground a fact
which fact, indeed, was simple –
                                    somemen who
though few and far between them firstly cracked
its shell, shocked me and made my eyes see through –
'twas this: the heart for art's sake must be wed
with all the mirageable might of love
and each must plight his truth with what was said
in words and achings full partaken of;
which means (as I'm concerned so far) begun
this great new miracle to tongue my soul
and I am summed with happiness that one
and one are two and two is onederful

so pleased am I that thus I must divine
my joyce at cummings on this sacred shrine

The Aerialist

The fling and fall of every swing he makes,
The risk he takes in staking all upon
A swoop through space, the certainty of grasp
And clasp that must efface all efforts, dupe
The gasping crowd with simulated slip.
He must combine the grip of limb with will
And grim unmoving vice of concentration.
Up there he has no other means of proving
Life's near-relation, luck; no second thought.
Struck from the poop of space, he is alone,
Owning what others sought – the pride of place
Above the tide of common fact below.
But is it so?
        His end is smartly drowned
In crisp applause, and slowly he'll descend
To join his other life upon the ground.

Antiphon

"Lord of the Seas and the Mighty Host" –
(Who cometh with the morning post).

"Lord of the Rocks and the Age of Men" –
(And after Age what happened then?)

"Lord of the Light and the Seven Stations" –
(Forgive us our meagre copulations).

"Lord of the Penny and Half-a-crown" –
(Who's put outside when the blind is down).

"Lord of the Psalm and Chromatic Scale" –
(Whose latest song is the siren's wail).

ENVOI

"Lord of Lords and King of Kings" –
(Who won't explain the sum of things).

Jingle

Give me the light to see the road.
Give me the road to follow.
Give me a thought or give me a word –
And I'll give you a poem to swallow.

Give me a sound to make a rhyme.
Give me a pen to write it.
Give me a soul that's filled with gloom –
And I'll give you a verse to light it.

Heaven's a land that's not in the sky
But pile-grown in your pocket.
Give me a chance to prove what I say –
And you won't be so ready to mock it.

Somehow, I know this of every man:
Each has his chosen sonnet.
Happy the one who has read his verse –
And modelled his life upon it.

Deep in a desert and drowned by the sun
Snuggles a cool oasis.
Give me a seat there beside you, pal –
And I'll take you to where that place is.

Suck up a tear of a love-lorn maid.
Mix it with blood of the dying.
Echo the cry of a new-born babe –
And then echo Death's shameless lying.

Take all the pathos in the world.
After the gay – take the tragic.
Each has a poem within my soul –
And each poem has its own kind of magic.

Yours is my voice. Mine is your life.
And I'll have this blasted world know it:
I'll be no jingling hoary bard –
I'll be a fool – or a poet.

So hand over that light and get off the road.
Here comes one man that's not hollow.
Give me the thought or just whisper the word –
And I'll say to the Devil "Come, Follow."

Prayer

From the Irish

O Christ of the seed
O autumn-Christ:
That we may be stored
In the barns of the Lord.

O Christ of the fish
O river-Christ:
In the nets of the Lord
May we find our reward.

From birth to growth
And from growth to death
The two hands, O Christ,
From over, beckon.

From birth to the end,
Isn't 'end' but re-birth,
Would we were
In the Halls of Grace.

The Stars Stand Up in the Sky

From the Irish

The stars stand up in the sky,
The sun and the moon are gone,
The sea had been drained till it's dry,
And his sway has forsaken the swan.
The cuckoo on top of the tree
Is repeating my lovely one's flight –
My girl of the curl flowing free,
She has gone – and I cry in my plight!

Three things through love I see:
Pain, and death, and sin;
And my mind is torturing me
With the sorrow my heart is in.
Oh why did I love her at all
And why did she wander away –
Ah, my girl, you're the cause of my fall,
May the Lord God forgive you some day.

Song of a Drowned Lover

From the Irish

My verse will sweep about your legs,
My rhyme will creep between your thighs;
Wracked, you will rise, as one who begs
Release with soft despairing eyes;
        But you will get no ease from me
        Nor from the syllabic sea.

The fish, the finger-finned fish,
With scale on scale your breasts will drape;
The strong green sea-weed's lazy swish
Will bind you fast without escape;
        And none, oh none at all, can save
        You from the consonantal wave.

Sink, sink, slowly sink
Down to my lonely ocean bed,
Where none will know or none will think
That you are gone, or lost, or dead.
        Cry not for help or ask not where;
        The tide will bring you to my lair.

How Sweet for the Birds

From the Irish

How sweet for the birds
Ascending so free,
And singing together
In the same tree.
Not so for my loved one
Or even for me,
For far from each other
The sunrise we see.

No wind is as fresh;
No lily as white;
No violin as sweet;
No sunshine as bright;
But better by far
Are her graces so light –
And O God in the Heavens,
Lessen my plight.

My Curse on the Sea

From the Irish

My curse on the sea,
It has torn us apart,
And it keeps me away
From the love of my heart.

I am left in this town
Alone with my sorrow,
And no sight of her face
Today or tomorrow.

My grief that I'm not
With my darling one fair
In the province of Leinster
Or wild County Clare.

My grief that I'm not
With the one I love best
On the deck of a ship
Sailing off to the west.

A bed of twigs
Was my bed last night,
But I cast them away
When the dawn was bright.

With my loved one beside me
How happy we'd rest,
My mouth to her mouth
And her breast to my breast.

The Unhappy Marriage

From the Irish

It's only twelve months since I married
And each day drags longer than a year;
I have no more desire for pleasure
Or for anything in particular.

On Monday the match was made –
Only a year ago last night –
And the main cause of my trouble
Was my own people's bad advice.

Oh I'm well and truly married –
That's a fate I've lived to regret;
But if I should catch a certain person
I promise you I'll break his neck.

I go into Mass of a Sunday
And all the young folk are there,
Then I catch sight of my love
And I can hardly see her for tears.

My hair is turning grey on me
And my strength is just about done,
If you don't come back to me quickly
I'll not last another month.

Oh my darling, darling loved one
I'd have been far better off dead
And lying there cold in my coffin
Before ever I said what I said.

The Fort of the Holy Cross

From the Irish

My home, my wife, my faith, my land,
From evil's grim design
O Lord, protect and keep them safe
With the Cross and its Holy Sign.

With death on the Cross you purchased all
Mankind and its luckless line,
From then till now how blessed is
That High and Holy Sign.

The mountains broke, the earth collapsed,
No sun was there to shine
When You were raised upon the back
Of the Cross and its Holy Sign.

On that account what man is there
Whose heart could cease to pine,
Or who restrain his tears before
The Cross's Holy Sign!

His reign is short who may be weak,
And certain his decline;
The Evil Spirit cannot march
With the hosts of the Holy Sign.

What a day of fear when Death's hand clasps
His neck like a creeping vine,
A terrible day it would be without
The Cross and its Holy Sign.

Woman Hot with Zeal

From the Irish of Seathrún Céitinn

Woman hot with zeal,
Your hands feeling me
Find my seed is dead
Though in bed we be.

Look! My hair is grey!
See the way my crotch
Shrinks before love's task!
Do not ask too much.

Take your mouth away,
I'll not play with fire
Lest your burning skin
Heat my thin desire.

Your hair's wild surprise,
Your two eyes ablaze,
Your white, budding breast
Twist with lust my gaze.

Do not shake your head,
Try, instead, discretion;
Flesh can flesh abide
Though denied possession.

Anything I'd do
For which you appeal
But that. That I cannot,
Woman hot with zeal.

The Coming of Christ

From the Irish of Pádraig Mac Píarais

I cleaned out my heart tonight
Like a woman who'd clean her house
At the news of her lover's return:
O Lover, don't pass my house!

I opened the door of my heart
Like a man who'd throw a feast
For his wandering son's return:
O Son, your return is sweet!

I Am Raftery

From the Irish of Antoine Ó Reachtabhra

I am Raftery, the poet,
Whose love's full of trust –
Whose eyes have no sight
And whose silence no lust.

Going back on my road
By the light of my heart,
Weary and tired
From finish to start.

With my back to the wall
Look at me here –
Playing to pockets
Empty and bare.

Repentance

From the Irish of Antoine Ó Reachtabhra

Creator of Adam, O King on High,
Who due regard to his sin must pay:
On the top of my voice to Thee I cry
Oh for Thy Grace I hope and pray.

Old I am like the withered clover,
From holiness I've turned my face.
I've fallen in sin now nine times over,
But God will not grudge me His store of grace.

The days escaped and the hedge not built
And the food Thou cherished rotted with blight;
O God of Goodness, forgive my guilt
And drench my eyes with Thy Holy Light.

I'm a useless stake thrown into a bush.
Or I'm like a boat that has lost its sail;
A boat that the rocks would crumble and crush,
Or for years would be driven before the gale.

So old I am that I'm next to death
And soon I'll be going to my grave;
But better than never that this last breath
Should speak with the Lord of the grace I crave.

I Saw You Naked

From the Irish of Pádraig Mac Píarais

I shielded my eyes
When I saw you naked.
I feared your beauty
Might make me turn traitor.

I covered my ears
When I heard you call me,
I feared your voice
Might make me a failure.

I hardened my heart
When you bent to kiss me,
I feared that your lips
Might keep me busy.

I shielded my eyes
And my ears I covered,
I hardened my heart
And my longing I murdered.

I turned my back
On the dream I had courted,
And I turned my face
To the deed before me.

I turned to the dream
That would be created –
To my destiny
And my death that waited.